For my birth...
from Pat.

H. L. Kasten.

Copyright © 1982 by Lone Pine Media Productions Ltd. and David Cunningham

First Printing 1982.

The Publishers:

Lone Pine Media Productions Ltd.
440, 10113 - 104 St.
Edmonton, Alberta

Printed and bound in Canada by
Douglas Printing Company
101, 11504 - 170 St.
Edmonton, Alberta

Typesetting and art by
Horizon Line Typecraft Ltd.
17220 - 107 Ave.
Edmonton, Alberta

Text and Sketches by Dave Cunningham

Edited by Grant Kennedy

ACKNOWLEDGEMENTS

Special thanks to:

Grant Kennedy and Steve Hume for seeing the value in a few thoughts and sketches.

My wife, Rebecca, for the encouragement, as well as all the hand lettering.

All the production staff for the patience and effort to accommodate my requests.

Scott and Darlene who's wedding invitations started me sketching and thinking.

ISBN 0-919433-10-3

THE BINDER

My grandfather saved everything, old lumber, an old binder ... over the years, every roller in the machine was pirated to fix the rig of one farmer neighbor or another. Eventually, I learned to see the value of old junk myself.

MAILBOXES

How I wished we had a road side mail box ···
with a little flag for the postman to flip up when
there was mail. Imagine living in the same place
long enough to have a box painted with the words
H.H. McGhee and son.

DEDICATION

I was born in Grande Prairie, Alberta. My family moved nearly every year of my life. One year we moved to Grandpa Cunningham's community. It was only 20 miles from Grandpa McGee's.

From the time I was 10 until I was 15 I visited or worked on my Grandpa McGee's farm during the summer. In the Fall and Winter I hunted and trapped with Grandpa Cunningham.

My Grandfathers had little in common except stubbornness. I was deeply affected by both of them, not so much through the skills and information they passed on but the gift of a sense of proportion. Today I freelance in the media and communications fields. I still often see things through their eyes.

These sketches and impressions were my world during those formative years. Some of them are gone. Some of them will endure.

Most of the experiences are my own, some have been drawn from the larger body of memory held in common by my extended family.

In particular, this is the interpreted world of my Grandfathers, and the book is dedicated to them.

GRANDPA MCGEE

Harvey moved to Alberta in 1904. He never gave up his American citizenship so he never became a Canadian. He believed in good old American know-how, though he never actually called it that. I don't think he believed in the personification of God, but he may have been waiting to see.

All men were equal in his eyes, at least until they proved themselves otherwise. He was generous to those who measured up and ruthless with those who didn't.

Mom once said that she thought maybe he'd shot a man in the States for forcing a lady off a boardwalk and into the street mud.

When he homesteaded in the community he became known as a man for firsts. He was the first to have running water, the first to have an automobile and the first to experiment with seeding the clouds with silver ions. (This was an attempt to prevent hail from forming. The theory was that ions would cause the moisture to fall before it could form hail stones.)

I think he believed he was part of a new landed gentry. No one ever proved him wrong. He built a cinder-surfaced tennis court for my aunts and uncles in 1939. The children were all encouraged to learn the arts and sciences from an early age.

He was gentle with women and tough on men. I never knew if I measured up in his eyes.

I learned the value of hard work and stubbornness from him. He was a man who kept his own council but was intrigued with anything new or unusual.

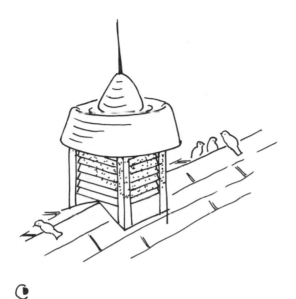

THE CUPOLA

There were always sparrows in the cupola...
In the summer, when the hay mow filled the loft,
you could climb up into it and catch them ... even
if you missed all the birds, you could still look
through the screen and slats, and see the whole
farm.

PAPA CUNNINGHAM

Walter didn't migrate here from anywhere. The Cunningham name came from Ireland, but Papa's people were always here. He came from a line of prominent and successful Cree people.

He was a devout and religious Catholic, who believed in Indian medicine and saw no conflict between the two. Even today I find myself talking to an animal before I shoot, though I seldom hunt anymore.

Papa Cunningham never had and never wanted much from the material world. A good gun, a fine pair of boots, maybe a knife with strong steel and a journey to take up in the morning. These might have been his basic needs.

The thing that Papa had was family. The laughter, teasing and tricks they inspired in each other completely changed my view of the world. They loved to wink at the priest in church or make up outrageous stories about one another.

He taught me the importance of understating or ignoring your predicament. I never heard him complain about the treatment that people sometimes gave him because of the color of his skin. I think he gained the respect of more people this way than anyone else I knew.

I met this grandfather of mine before I knew my father. When I was young I hunted alone in the coulees where I met him and his sons. They adopted me.

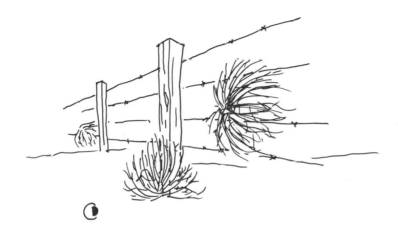

TUMBLEWEEDS

· · · set in motion by the ever present dust and wind · · · I always thought they were actually animals · · · Just to see one bound across the road in front of the head lights · · ·

Table of Contents

	Page		Page
Making Do On The Prairie	13	Chigee Pulldo Mudhen	
The Lonesome Trail	15	Snowbirds & Sparrows	
Sheep		Quill Pen	32
Telling Time		Whistle	
Alkali Salt Licks		Fans & Decorations	33
Crossed Rail Fence	16	Ta Goy Wim Na Na	36
Stacked Rail Fence		Vegetable Vendors	37
Hold Downs		Bull Berries	
Dead Man	17	Prickly Pear Cactus	38
Post Holes		Cactus Berries	
Corner Posts		Silver Willow	
Snubbing Post	19	Dandelions	
Maggots		Pig Weed	
Gestation of Pigs		Dried Apples	39
White Wash		Summer Kitchen	
		Sauerkraut	
Coulees	22	Bannock	40
Beaver		Johnny Cake	42
Tanning Hides	24	Cattail Root	
Cleaning a Gun		Soap Sunday & Lent	43
		Buckbrush Broom	
Rabbits	27		
Rabbit Stew	29	Butter	45
Hawk's Nest	30	Butter Press	46
Blowing Up A Craw			
A Little Village		Kinnikinik	51
Flappers	31	Calamus Root	52

	Page		Page
Grandma's Cures	53	Egg Toss	69
Pine Tea		Sports Day	
Sage Brush Liniment		Mouth Music	
Spruce & Pine Pitch		Hotel Bars	71
Molasses		Halloween	
Mustard Plasters		The Oldest Joke	
Blue Stone			
Goose Grease		The Mine	76
Tobacco		Bone Coal	78
Plantain		Rocks	
Kerosene		Polish Potatoes	
Tea Bags		Splitting Fieldstone	79
Dried Mint			
		Snake Hills	82
Box Car Sleighs	57	Bull Snakes	
Bobs		Making A Knife	87
Ground Squirrels	58	Smithing	
Pocket Knives	59	Forge Welding	88
Shingle Arrows		Woodstain	89
Fire Crackers	60	Shellac	
Black Powder		Leather Hinges	
Goldeye	63	Divining	93
Clams & Crayfish		Artesian Wells	94
Sinkers	64	Cutting Ice	95
Smoked Fish	65	Ice Pits	98
Clay Baking			

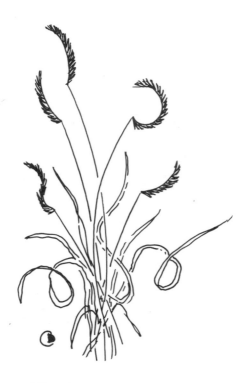

PRAIRIE WOOL

    It's a kind of grass native to Alberta · · · once
it was everywhere. · · As grasses go, it's extremely
high in nutrients. But it couldn't survive intensive
grazing · · · Now it's rare to find a meadow of it.

MAKING DO . . .
. . . ON THE PRAIRIE

A lot of books have been written about the great central plains. Much has been written about homesteader folk-lore and survival. It seems that many authors have written around the unique forms of prairie life. There are no stories of oak trees or sour gum in this book because they are not part of the folklore of our semi-desert northern region.

There is a unique mix of Native and European ways that will not be found in books published in the States.

The life was tough, extremely hard and occasionally very rewarding. By the time I was born it was almost part of the past. Fortunately the prairies have their own peculiarities and even today you find a walking plow and a four-wheel-drive diesel being used on the same farm.

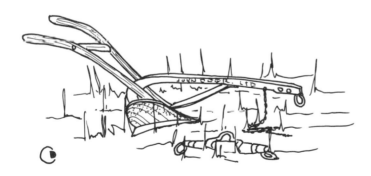

People on the prairie were quick to take up any new method or machine if it was of use to them. But they gave up old ways and ideas very slowly.

This is how I found the prairie of my youth, hopelessly confusing but exactly as it should be.

I hope you find strength and beauty in prairie life also.

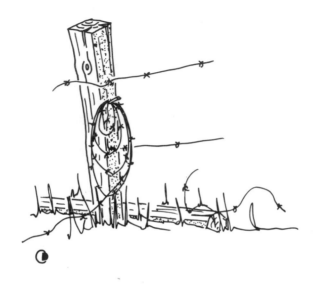

CEDAR POSTS

    In the spring, my father would help me look
for an old cedar fence post... It had to be cedar...
only cedar splits into long light laths. What did we
do with the lath? ... Why, it made wonderful
ribs for kites.

THE LONESOME TRAIL

The lonesome trail is wherever there's a cowboy riding fence, and nothing else.

SHEEP

I have a prairie man's bias against sheep. I never saw a stupider, more high strung or sillier animal. They've got no sense. They'll run themselves to death at the drop of a hat, or they'll fall down in a swoon of fright. Most diseases kill them and they're always likely to have fleas, lice or ticks, no matter how you dip them. And to top it all off, I don't like mutton. Any sheep I've seen raised successfully were let run free out on the leases. They seemed to fare better if they never ran over the same ground twice.

TELLING THE TIME

Once when we were hunting we came across an old shepherd's camp. Beside the remains of the cook fire little stones were laid out in rows of seven. That guy had been at the same camp for five weeks my Grampa said.

ALKALI SALT LICKS

Deer and our own livestock could often be seen licking the white deposit in a dried pond. They were after the salt. These sloughs existed wherever water ran in but couldn't run out. Small ones dried out by mid-summer and seemed to concentrate the salt.

CROSSED RAIL FENCE

You have to admit it looks awful nice, but living where we lived it was totally impractical to construct. We didn't have the timber.

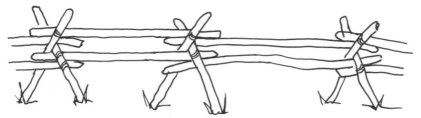

STACKED RAIL FENCE

Sometimes if there was a particularly easy route for livestock to go around a regular fence, like a slough or a creek, we'd stack fence rails up to make a kind of barrier for the animals. It didn't always work and it took a lot of timber and a lot of time to build.

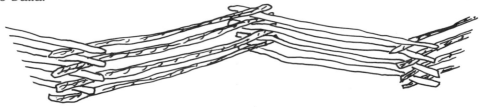

HOLD DOWNS

I've watched farmers tighten up a fence strand by tying a rock to the wire close to the staple. This pulled the fence taut again alright, but if there were many on one fence it looked like the fence was growing stone pumpkins.

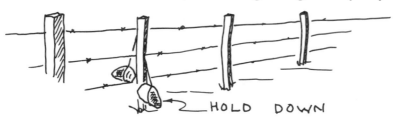

HOLD DOWN

DEAD MAN

To brace the end of a fence line the men
tied a strand of barbed wire around a
big rock or post and buried it; that
would hold a fence up as well
and for as long as any
tree could.

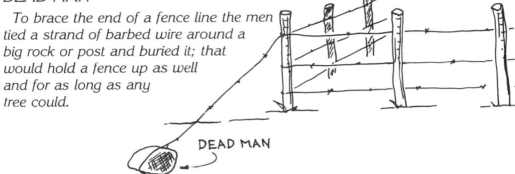

DEAD MAN

POST HOLES

Most people on the prairie know that you don't dig post holes, you pound them. Gramp made this look simple. He just lined up a post and took his maul and smacked it on the head until it was buried its required depth. If the ground was hard and dry as rock then and only then would he use a little water to soften the ground at the start. He was still pounding fences like this when he was 72, and he was still faster and better at it than anyone I ever saw. I don't believe I've ever seen either of my grandfathers dig a post hole.

CORNER POSTS

Corners are always a problem in fencing and this is one of the most common

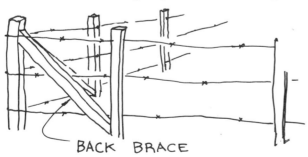

BACK BRACE

ways of making them hold solid. Just brace the corner back to the next post on each side. It's the top of the corner post you're worried about, so the brace runs from the corner top to the next post's bottom.

OLD BARN. DEAD WINDMILLS

Farmers seem to have a reluctance to pull down
an old barn once it's past using. They are mostly left
to fall down and retire gracefully back into the earth.
The buildings are memories of the struggle to homestead
on the lonely prairie, and they can't destroy them.

THE STILE

We had some Dutch neighbors and they had a stile. It always seemed very exotic to me · · · a very interesting and elaborate way to get over a fence · · · even better than a Texas gate.

SNUBBING POST

I used to wonder what they used the post that stands alone in the middle of a breaking corral for. It was called a snubbing post and it seemed you could never hold a horse to it if the horse had other ideas. This is true. However, a man who knows what he's doing can use the leverage and mechanical advantage it gives him to lasso and snub a horse in a very short time.

I only saw it used once, and when the cowboy had snubbed the terrified one-year-old to the pole (I was as sick and terrified as the horse) the poor thing was tired out and choking on the rope until the wind rattled in its chest.

MAGGOTS

Maggots have gone out of fashion since I was a kid. Times when a horse or a dog got gangrene from a wound or frost bite, gramps would scrape maggots into the dead flesh. It was called proud flesh. The maggots wouldn't eat live flesh, but ate up rotting tissue and seemed to disinfect the wound. He told me that the maggots did a better job of cleaning the wound than he could, plus he didn't have to run the risk of cutting good tissue with a knife.

THE GESTATION OF PIGS

If you asked a farmer from around home how long it takes a sow to farrow, he'd probably laugh and say three months, three weeks, three days and three o'clock in the morning.

WHITEWASH

Fresh whitewash kills ticks and fleas. Gramps painted the roost in the chicken coop with it. When the flock perched for the night their bodies activated the paint and it rose up through them. This way they fumigated themselves. Gramp's chickens never had scabs or bites on the skins.

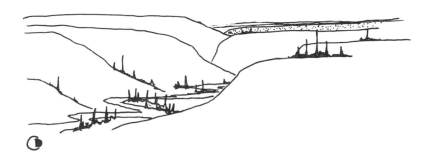

THE COULEE

The Red Deer River valley stretches away almost to the Saskatchewan border ··· I've heard people say it's empty, barren ··· but I've seen over a hundred deer disappear down its slopes on a fall evening.

COULEES

Back home we called all the valley and canyons 'coulees'. I never knew why. For a long time I thought it had something to do with the Chinese that had been brought in to build the railway. Sort of as a tribute to their efforts; misguided, but touching.

Actually it comes from the French word 'couler', which means to flow. So there you have it, it's got nothing to do with the Chinese, and everything to do with the French Canadian fur trade.

BEAVER

The first time my grandfather skinned a beaver for sale to the Hudson Bay Company, someone told him "Leave as much meat on as you can. They like them with lots of meat". So, grandpa took his first hides in to the fur-buying station with only the bones and insides removed. They laughed him out of the store.

That's how my grandfather became one of the best fur dressers in the country. Being made a fool of can drive a man to success. By the time I learned to dress hides from him, he

thinnest peltries
He could take a hide
worth maybe $20.00
and dress it with such
bid $30.00 for it.
board for coyotes,
weasels, squirrels and
but our main source of

Beaver learn
easy to trap on the first
ond. Their favorite
almost can't resist the
or castor.

STRETCHING BOARDS

made the cleanest,
anywhere in the West.
that was going to be
in anyone else's hands
care that he would be
We had a stretching
rats (muskrats), mink,
the occasional fox,
furs was beaver.

quick. They are quite
try, but not the sec-
color is red, and they
scent of licorice, anise

BEAVER

We sometimes shot them from the creek bank, though not very often. Your shot had to be very carefully placed, either an eye, ear or nose opening. If the shell entered the eye or ear it went into the brain and kept the pelt free of a hole. If you hit a beaver on the nose he would not dive. But a body shot was a bad shot, even if it killed him. You would never see the animal again. Beaver will drown on the bottom rather than surface badly hurt.

The law in my family was that if you shot a beaver you didn't leave the creek until you found him. We killed them, but we couldn't abide them suffering because of us. At one time or another I've seen most of my family reduced to tears over a wounded animal that got away, but wasn't likely to survive.

I shot my first beaver when I was 10. My papa and I were about 10 miles from home and it was getting dark. It was a young lone bachelor, and I killed him cleanly. He weighed about 45 pounds. Not a blanket, but a good size. I was excited and very pleased.

In our family, you haul what you kill. After about an hour of trying to pack the beaver and my old army .22, I was dragging. Papa had been on the other side of the river and had to walk around to a bridge in order to meet me. When he arrived and saw a 10 year-old boy lugging an animal almost two-thirds his weight, he picked us both up. With me on one shoulder and my beaver on the other, he carried us home.

TANNING HIDES

Jose was our baby sitter — sort of a live-in nanny. Jose always tanned her own moose and deer hides after she scraped all the hair off the skin and trimmed all the fat. She rubbed the hide with a combination of brains and urine and bark off the black alder tree. The tree bark works like a pigment or dye and gives the hide a reddish-brown color. The Indians call the tree Ma Mee Chuse (The tree that's no good for nothing) which is funny because they use it for a lot of things. Sometimes Jose soaked the hide for days in a watered-down version of this mixture.

HIDE STRETCHED
WITH NAILS & PLYWOOD

Jose would not chew the cleaned hide with her teeth. If you wanted it softer you could chew it yourself.

The other side of my family also tanned hides. After the hide was cleaned, scraped and washed they painted it with a thick mixture of borax, saltpeter, salt and flour. Then they rolled it up and let the hide cure for about 10 days after which they washed it several times, finally producing a soft and very white hide.

DADS OLD 25/20.

CLEANING A GUN

If you have a gun that doesn't have a removable bolt it's difficult to see if you have cleaned all the spent powder out of the barrel. Open the breach and place a piece of white paper in it at an angle then look down the barrel. The white paper reflects light into the barrel and is usually enough to see by. You can clean it now to your satisfaction.

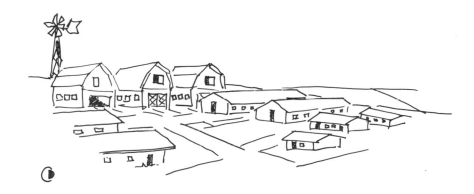

HUTTERITE COLONIES

They were all around us, but they didn't like company much · · · why they let our family hunt on their property, I don't know · · · maybe it was because we asked.

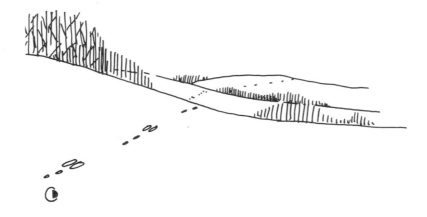

RABBITS

I got my first rifle when I was 12 · · · on Christmas Day · · · It was a miracle, I had only saved half of the $29.50 price tag - my parents put in the rest · · · I went out and shot four Jack rabbits that same day.

RABBITS

Our family shot a lot of rabbits. They often filled the stew pot. Any extras were fed to the dogs or sold to the mink rancher. We learned a lot of tricks about these animals. I don't imagine they are any secret, but who knows? Here are a few:

If a rabbit is running away from you too fast, whistle a couple of times real low. It will probably stop to listen, and that will give you a shot.

If you can hear a bunny in the bush but he won't flush, stop kind of sudden. A rabbit gets nervous pretty fast if he doesn't know what's happening. If he can't figure out why you've stopped, often as not he will bolt. (This works even better with some upland-game birds.)

Of course we were all able to track a rabbit trail and locate a Jack by simply following it. You have to remember, though, that when he runs he lands with his back feet first and his front feet last. The tracks look like they are going in the opposite direction.

Prairie rabbits go through a cycle that devastates their population. The disease comes when they seem to be

everywhere. You can tell they are sick when you skin them. There will be small pea-sized cysts and boils in the flesh and under the skin. This is a good time to sell them to the mink man. I don't know what would happen if you ate one, because we never did.

RABBIT STEW

My Aunt had a big white cat named Rowdy Yates, named after a chuck wagon outrider my grandfather knew. (Both the cat and the rider were as cocky as could be.) This cat used to sit outside the kitchen window ledge and watch the family eat supper. He was an awful distraction because he followed the meal's progress so closely, and the kids were always trying to feed him.

One day we were invited over for supper. My grandfather had shot a couple of rabbits and they were already cooking. My younger brother and a cousin wanted to know what kind of birds we were having for supper. There seemed to be eight drumsticks and no breast meat. Before my aunt could answer, gramps said that we were eating Rowdy Yates. Immediately seven young pairs of eyes went to the window ledge. The cat was gone. Well, that finished it. The kids wouldn't eat a mouthful and the younger ones were crying. My aunt was fuming fit to be tied.

It took quite a while but the kids finally decided that grandpa had been fooling about the cat and calmed down enough to finish the meal. The last laugh was on him though, because that cat never did show up again.

Another time the kids made such a fuss was when gramps came home one early spring with a single bush rabbit and said he had shot the Easter Bunny by mistake. This was two or three days before Easter. There was an awful howling that time, too.

MAGPIE NESTS AND CROW'S EGGS

We robbed the eggs and fledglings for the bounty. An egg could break in your pocket, so I used to put them in my mouth while I climbed down · · · I've eaten a few raw crow eggs in my day

HAWK'S NEST

A hawk will build her nest in the same place year after year. Each nest is built on top of the remains of the last one. Eventually this can lead to a nest 10 or 11 feet high in a tree that's not much higher. I managed to steal an owl or hawk fledgling every year and raise it.

BLOWING UP A CRAW

This is not something that our parents were ever very thrilled about. If we managed to get the craw out of a pheasant or a duck without tearing it, we'd blow it up and tie it at both ends. This made us a little volleyball until it got dried out. It was useless then.

A LITTLE VILLAGE

One time my grandfather took his daughters hunting with him. This was something that didn't usually happen. They had a successful day's hunt and it was left to the girls to pluck and clean the ducks for supper. Little girls are queezy, or maybe they didn't know how. They managed to pluck the birds all right, but they weren't up to taking the insides out. When gramps pulled the lid off the cooking pot he was surprised to see the rear ends of seven little teal ducks steaming away. He laughed until he cried. "Just like a little village in the wintertime!" he said.

FLAPPERS

To us flappers weren't young ladies, they were young ducks. We ran a constant battle with the game warden over these quackers. Since we could catch them with our hands or shoot them with a sling shot, and they were just big enough to eat over the camp fire, we didn't think the warden should interfere.

When one of us stumbled on a moulting flock it was a bonanza. Mallard drakes lose their big feathers after the spring mating. This makes them unable to fly. They usually hold out together in a secluded pond until their feathers grow back. These full grown ducks had much more good meat on them so we would return to their spot every day until we either became bored with roast duck or the creatures fled on webbed feet to the creek.

CHIGGEE PULLDO MUD HEN

A greeb by any other name would taste as bad, their eggs, though, were a great treat. They're so easy to find too because they build their nest in open water.

SNOW BIRDS AND SPARROWS

French and Italian people in our community used to have a taste for sparrows and snow birds.

For catching the little white snow birds they made traps that looked like the heads of two tennis rackets tied together. Flocks of birds would be lured into the trap with piles of grain. The wire mesh on the tennis rackets was spaced so the little birds could get their feet between the strands, but were not able to extract them.

To bag a quota of sparrow was much easier. They'd spread grain on the ground, wait until a large flock landed to dine, and open up on them with a load of No. 10 shot.

To clean these little guys was simple. All you had to do was rip the breast off and throw the rest away. This meal was thought to be real fancy and made people feel as though they were dining like kings and queens of Europe.

FEATHERS
A QUILL PEN OR A WHISTLE

After one of my Gran's turkeys attacked one of the cousins and nearly got her, my grandfather butchered the lot and said we'd never keep them again. Before that though we could scour the barn for their moulted wing feathers to make quill pens and whistles.

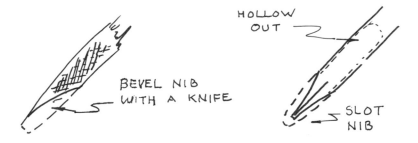

HOLLOW OUT

BEVEL NIB WITH A KNIFE

SLOT NIB

The pens were quite simple to make. After slicing the tip of the feather on an angle the pithy inside had to be removed. The only part that was a bit tricky was slitting an ink groove down the middle of the newly formed point. If it was too tight the nib didn't hold enough ink and dried up before you could write your name.

It's a lot harder to make a whistle but, as kids, most of our efforts ran in this direction. First you cut off the plume end, then hollowed out the rest of the quill. You had to be careful to leave the pith in the plume end except for an air passage

at the top. When this was completed all that was left to do was make a slot in the top. They almost never worked well and when they did the sound produced was extremely high and made the dogs howl. It was very much the same as a willow whistle.

FANS AND DECORATIONS

The other side of my family used feathers quite differently. A goose or wild turkey wing could be stretched and dried to make a fan or a duster. The thing I liked best though was to stretch and dry the tail of a ruffed grouse or bush partridge. They can be fanned out in a neat half circle and are so beautiful they don't need to have a purpose. This has to done before the flesh dries. I always attached them to a cardboard backing and used straight pins to hold them open.

CACTUS

When we went tobogganing on the prairie, we always avoided south exposures in the coulees. Since they were more arid than the protected north exposure, that's where the cactus grew. Invariably, if you upset your toboggan, it would be in the middle of a snow covered cactus patch · · · A memorable experience not to be repeated!

PRICKLY PEAR CACTUS

There weren't a lot of cactus around the home coulee but one of gramps' cousins lived in the southern part of the province and he had lots of it. He torched them in the fall, burning off the spines, after discovering the cattle liked them once the stickles were gone.

CACTUS BERRIES

We ate two different kinds. One was a small, fruity bulb that grew under the yellow flowers on the prickly pear. This is the cactus in the picture.

The other I don't remember so well. Its leaves hugged the ground. The berries, which ripened late in the Fall, were clustered in the dish-like centre of this plant. They looked and tasted like over-ripe gooseberries.

SILVER WILLOW BERRIES

My dad and I ate these as we hunted, or rather we chewed on the pulpy flesh. On the inside there was a large striped stone or pit. It was actually quite attractive.

When the Catholic Fathers first began to convert Indians to the Faith the natives made rosaries from them. I'm sure they were already used as beads long before this though.

DANDELIONS

The root roasted and dried can be ground for coffee. The blossoms make dandelion wine and, of course, the tender young greens are excellent when added to salad.

PIG WEED

My mother picked this in the spring to supplement our winter diet. It tastes like asparagus stock. Once you get to know a few plants, it seems almost everything that grows is edible.

TA GOY WIM NA NA

This is stuff only an old Indian could like. Most people are perfectly happy with making chokecherry wine or jelly from these plentiful berries; not my grandparents. They would take a washtub of picked and cleaned berries down to the butcher. He ground up the lot, pits and all. Then they were cooked and mixed with equal parts of fresh rendered lard.

It's supposed to be a real treat, kind of like eating bacon drippings laced with blackberry jam and cut with pea-sized road gravel.

We had to eat it as a spread on toast, sometimes as a cold appetizer or snack, but the most disgusting way of all was to fry it. My grandfather especially liked it this way. It looks like nothing so much as bear shit, and we kids called the stuff ca ca balls. You can keep it through winter if you put it in sealers or dry it into balls about the size of a large meat ball.

My great grandma made this preserve by drying it on a blanket over a woodshed. All the kids in town used to call it "granny Cunningham's chewin' tobaccy". It was a big joke to distract her somehow and then steal it. More than one kid came home with his mouth all purple from chewin' and hawkin' granny's chewin' tobaccy.

THE VEGETABLE VENDORS

In the Fall, Hutterite families descended on our community hawking their produce. Cucumbers, potatoes and sometimes hand-picked wild berries. An elderly gentleman led the ladies door-to-door offering their wares. They in turn had the younger children in tow.

Later, after the selling was over the ladies could be found in the hardware store. They talked and giggled and pointed out the cloth they wished to buy. It was always black or dark blue, with polka dots. Pretty somber stuff.

BULL BERRIES

These are really small and fragile red berries that grow on a low shrub that has the look of a hawthorn and a silver willow combined. If you try to pick them by hand it's more or less a hopeless task. For starters it takes about a thousand just to fill the bottom of a berry pail and for another thing the amount of pressue you have to use to pick them is usually enough to burst the fruit. You can't pick them, that's all there is to it.

There is a way to harvest them though and we loved to amaze visitors with the tubfulls we could lug home.

The secret is to wait until the first frost, and carry a big stick. We would spread a tarp out underneath a tree loaded with fruit, and then bang the living daylights out of the trunk. Once the berries have been slightly frozen they fall off the tree all by themselves. We could harvest an entire hillside like this in about an hour.

CANNING

If mom hadn't canned, we wouldn't have had
fruit in the winter · · · raspberries, saskatoons,
cranberries, crabapples · · · and rhubarb. Rhubarb
with cherries, rhubarb with carrots · · · rhubarb
with anything.

DRIED APPLES

You can dry your own apples just by cutting them into thin slices and laying them in the sun. If you want them to keep through the winter they should be sulfured.

Put all of your apple slices on a rack in a barrel, place a light cloth over the top and burn a teaspoon of sulfur in the bottom of the barrel. (There is always a lump or two of the yellow stuff to be found along the railway track.)

The apples will keep from moulding all winter long. I'm told the sulfur might even be good for you.

SUMMER KITCHEN

In August when the days got so terribly hot gran would make grampa move the wood stove outside under a lean-to. Later they got a new coal and wood stove for inside so the wood stove stayed outside in the Fall and Winter too, for canning and rendering.

SAUERKRAUT

A lot of things can be preserved by controlling the way that they spoil. This is true of wine and cheese. I hate to say it, but it's also true of sauerkraut. Gran had a huge crock for it. This crock held over 50 gallons and was set permanently behind the door to the cellar. It was too large to ever think of moving; God knows what it weighed when it was full.

She filled the crock with layers of shredded green cabbage and layers of salt. Then she drowned the cabbage in water with just a little vinegar in it. There it sat, stinking and fermenting until one day it was salty and sharp as a pickle. We now had sauerkraut. I liked to eat it with boiled potatoes, add a little cured ham and it was perfect.

BANNOCK

All the Indians in Western Canada think they invented bannock, my family included. In fact, no one likes tea and bannock better than my family. Not even the Scots, and they are the ones who brought the tradition to Canada when they first came here. Indian and Metis families have made it ever since, and seeing as how that's just about 300 years ago now, I think we can lay claim to it.

FRIED BANNOCK

We made bannock in three different ways. The easiest and quickest way is to make fried bannock. You don't put any lard or shortening in the dough because the bread is fried in a skillet with about 3/4 of an inch of oil or grease. I always cut the dough into small portions, and I really like to add raisins or dried fruit. You're best to eat them right away, although good ones are fine when they're cold.

The hardest way to make bannock is on a stick. This time you have to make the recipe with more water so it will stick to your willow branch. If you make it too sticky the dough will kind of harden up like old glue. The best thing about this is you don't need any utensils. When we had killed a rabbit for lunch and spit it, we would put our bannock on a couple of spits right beside the rabbit. The whole meal didn't require a pot. Bill Carrier even used a flour sack to mix it on, so he didn't need a mixing bowl.

BANNOCK
ON A
STICK

BANNOCK

The best way to make bannock is just to bake it. If you have an oven you can cook it like baking powder biscuits. If you're out in the bush, you cook it in a skillet. First you bake the bottom by holding the pan flat over hot coals. When it's nearly cooked through, you brown the top by propping up the pan by the handle and turning the bannock until it's all nicely golden brown.

If you flour the pan first, the bannock won't stick, and if any dirt or ashes fall on the top you can easily blow them off. (Don't brush them, or they will smear.) When the bannock is done, take some butter and glaze the tops. This makes it look even better.

Here's Grandma's Basic Bannock Recipe:
  4 cups white flour
  1 large tablespoon baking powder
  1 tablespoon lard
  1 teaspoon salt
  1 1/2 cups water (This is not the rule, once you've made it a couple of times
       you'll know when you've got enough.)

JOHNNY CAKE

When we first moved near to my grandparents I had never seen corn meal before. It was the stuff of nursery rhymes and fairy tales. I didn't realize people ate it in real life. My gran made it for us the first time for breakfast, and served it with butter and syrup. It's been one of my favorite meals ever since; any time of the day.

This is her recipe:

JOHNNY CAKE

1/4 c. sugar   1 c. milk
1 egg   1/4 c. butter
1/2 tsp. soda   1 c. cornmeal
1/2 c. flour   1 tsp. cream of
                        tartar

(Bake in a moderate oven.)

The term Johnny Cake comes from an earlier name "Journey Cake". It kept well for a long time, so it was good to travel with. My ma told me this.

CATTAIL ROOT

Harvest and dry the roots from cattails. They can be ground up and mixed with flour to stretch your supply. The pollen from the spike is also a good flour substitute.

SOAP SUNDAY AND LENT

My grandma made her own soap from lye, tallow and a little borax and ammonia. Sometimes she still does. It's the nicest, cleanest-smelling soap I've ever used. At one time she even leached her own lye from wood ash, but now she just buys it at the hardware.

This was her recipe for homemade soap:

- dissolve 1 cup of lye in 1 quart of water.
- melt 6 pounds of tallow.
- dissolve 1 cup of ammonia and 1/2 cup borax in a little water.
- mix together until creamy and white.
- scent it with lemon if you like.
- pour into a cloth-lined box.
- - cut into hand-sized blocks when cooled.

Gran always made soap as penance for Lent. Since it had to be made anyway, it was the perfect time to match religious and household duties. I always liked this matchup.

BUCKBRUSH BROOM

I never saw this but my pa says that grandma used to cut buckbrush into lengths and tie it around a stick or an old piece of broom handle. During the depression that was as close to a broom as she got.

MILK TREES
    Not many of the neighbors were dairy men ·· ·
everyone kept a few cows though. You could see the
milk pails winking brightly for miles, hung out in
the sun to dry.

THE CREAM SEPARATOR

I understand how these things work, · · · but I still don't believe it. You put whole milk in here and churn it around · · · then the lighter cream comes out on top, skim milk below.

BUTTER

Anyone can make butter. You only need one ingredient, and that's cream. There are many gadgets for churning butter: blenders, food processors, butter churns, butter barrels. They all work fine.

The simplest way to make butter is almost absurd, it's so easy. All you need is a quart sealer and a pint of cream. First put the cream in a sealer and screw the lid on tight. Now you just shake it until it turns to butter. That's all there is to it. Some people drain off the whey and pat the butter dry. This helps to keep it longer. Others like to add a little salt, but none of that is necessary for a small amount.

BUTTER PRESS

My grandmother sold her butter in town so she needed to press it into one-pound packets. To do this she used butter paper and a butter press. Nobody seems to put butter into paper anymore, but some kinds of margarine and lard still come that way. It's quite tough, slightly waxed, and usually white or translucent.

Before you use a butter press you have to soak it in cold water so the butter won't stick. You should also remember never to paint or oil the press because then the cold water can't get into the wood.

The next thing you have to do is line the box with a butter paper. Once you've got that done, you just fill the whole thing with fresh butter. Take a knife and trim the extra flush with the bottom of the box.

Now you turn the whole thing upright and push the plunger. Out will come a neat one pound package of butter. (That's called printing a pat.) All that's left to do is finish wrapping it up in the paper.

My gran had particularly good butter. The grocer who sold for her would pass off butter from other farms as being hers. She didn't like that because he sold poor butter and pretended it was from our farm. He also knew that he could get a higher price if people thought it was gran's. To let people know a package was hers, she had a little mold that said "Turtle Back Farm", with a little turtle right on the plunger. Then every time she printed a pound of butter her trademark was already right on it.

CEREAL

There's a town south of here called Cereal. It's nothing more than a line of elevators on a straight stretch of railway in the middle of the empty prairie · · · My brother and I thought it was so strange · · · to name a town after breakfast food.

GRANARIES
        People who visited the farm always thought
all the little houses were so cute · · · We
thought they were nuts. A granary was a
granary – as far as we were concerned!

GRAIN

No it's not wheat, it's barley. Wheat doesn't have much of a beard... My uncle used to get quite excited if the combine broke the husk off of the Kernal during threshing. The Pool paid the best price for malt barley and the Kernals and husk had to be intact.

SLEEPY JOHN

    I picked wildflowers for Mom all season long;
crocuses, flowering crab apple, buffalo beans, lilacs,
prairie lilies and indian paint brush. When the
weather turned, there were cat tails, grain stalks
and dry frosted leaves.

KINNIKINIK

There's a dozen things called kinnikinik but here I'm talking about local Indian's tobacco. Western Canadian Indians never had real Ontario or Virginia leaf. In fact the tobacco they smoked was not made from leaves at all. Papa said Indians smoked lots of different plants for their power and medicine. Kinnikinik was mostly for enjoyment.

On the prairie kinnikinik is the pithy inner bark of the red willow tree. (You get to it by removing the dark red outer bark layer.) The inner bark scrapes off in little curls that look a bit like hand-rubbed cut plug. The little curls should be dried and mixed with a few blueberry leaves. Blueberry leaves alone do not make good kinnikinik because they send out a very hot, uncomfortable smoke. That's why it's good to mix them with the red willow bark. They help to keep it burning.

A friend of mine once left me a can of plain blueberry leaves and after I had smoked about four pipe-fulls my throat was burnt. I never smoked another charge. Red willow bark on its own isn't so bad.

Some people think you get stoned if you smoke enough kinnikinik. It isn't true.

CALAMUS ROOT (RAT ROOT)

This is the most medicinal plant in North America. It has a use in the treatment of almost every ailment a person can get. It is a root stalk that grows under slough grass and it looks like ar-rowhead plants with spikey green cattails. The root is like a skinny ginger root. The taste is like ginger too, except for the un-mistakeable flavour and burn of camphor.

It can be boiled and applied like a wash or concentrated salve. One way is to hold a small piece about the size of a pea under your lip and suck on it until it goes to pulp.

You can use it for colds and coughs, sore throats and sinus problems, morning sickness, upset stomach, ulcers, flu and fevers. It will relieve a toothache or muscle pain from overwork. It can be applied as a compress or washed on burns, stings, blisters and boils. It's also very effective against eczemas, especially those caused by ner-vous and emotional strain.

I can't think of any more just now, but we all carry a piece around with us and offer it as a cure for any affliction. Every year someone discovers another use for it. It is one of the finest old Indian medicines to be handed down for us to save and protect.

Calamus is a type of iris and was known as a herbal cure in the time of the pharaohs. It grows well on the Nile River.

GRANDMA'S NATURAL CURES, POTIONS AND RECIPES

Most of her recipes were made from everyday things from the house or farm.

PINE TEA is good for what ails you, especially when you haven't got fresh vegetables in winter.

SAGE BRUSH root can be boiled up to make a liniment for muscle pain. It will make you sick if you drink it.

SPRUCE AND PINE PITCH can be used to disinfect and cover small cuts and scratches, or even to dress a cleaned wound.

MOLASSES can be used for just about everything, simply by the tablespoon or in hot tea.

MUSTARD PLASTERS were surely a case of the cure being at least as bad as the disease. Most people got better in self-defense. Gran used it to cure whooping cough, common colds, pneumonia and chest pains from tuberculosis.

It was just a paste of Keen's dry prepared mustard mixed with flour and water. This was spread between layers of gauze and old strips of linen. The whole works went on your chest. There it either burned the ailment out of you or the skin off your chest! Grandma swore by it.

KALSAMINE, BLUE STONE AND COPPER SULFATE were used to get rid of bed bugs and lice.

GOOSE GREASE was not really a cure, but an everyday lotion. It was thought to be the best ointment for babies bottoms. Grandma always saved the renderings.

SOME MORE OF GRANDMA'S NATURAL CURES, POTIONS AND RECIPES

TOBACCO was actually one of gramps' remedies for ringworm. He'd chew the tobacco up first, then grab a kid tight (nobody would sit still for this) and rub the awful mess over the infected area. It got remarkable results!

PLANTAIN was the best thing going for a bee-sting. Even today, with special things on the market, I still use a poultice of dried and boiled plantain leaves. Not only does it take down the swelling of a sting, but it also relieves other itches and scratches.

A bee's stinger will usually still be in you when the rest of the bee has gone. It's better to scrape it off instead of pulling it out because there is a bulb of poison at the top of the stinger.

KEROSENE. It's remarkable what people thought kerosene could do, outside of burning. My father's family put it in their hair to kill the lice and bedbugs they brought home from school. Once in a while they were even made to drink a tablespoonful to kill worms. Bruises or cuts were often disinfected with it.

TEA BAGS were used on a stye or to cure pink eye.

DRIED MINT was considered a medical potion but we drank a lot of it with regular tea. This was one herb I was particularly good at finding. The smell is faintly skunk-like when crushed or picked.

SKUNK-OIL. Once a medicine man came to my dad's house to cure the family of whooping cough. He brought a scent sack from a skunk for this purpose. It was stored in a pouch inside four tightly sealed tins and still the smell filled the house the minute he entered. Each of the children had to take a drop of oil on their tongue. Dad said it burned and made his eyes water and his nose run. He thought he would die, but it got the cough first and left him healthy and smelly.

THE WATER TOWER

    Ours didn't look like the ones in the movies · · · we used to tell new kids that it still serviced a real steam locomotive · · · truth was, none of us had ever seen anything but the diesel electric

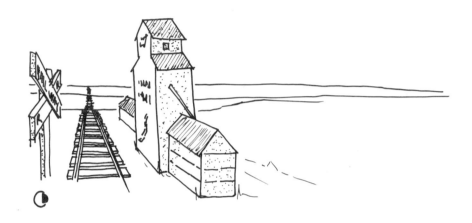

THE RAILWAY

    The tracks were like a private hi-way for kids and trains · · · We walked everywhere on them · · · It was an acquired skill— the ties were too far apart to take two at a time, and too close together to step on every one.

BOX CAR SLEIGHS

Everything a kid needs for a good sleigh can be pilfered from a grain car in about five minutes. The plank hoarding that seals the grain doors is thick and makes fine runners and cross-pieces. To make the runners even slicker you want steel rods along the bottom. Brake-rod dowels are just the right size and are held in place with only a cotter pin. There is enough rod on a boxcar to outfit a good bobsled. No one ever seemed to get hurt, but today I wonder what it meant to have one of the box cars with no brakes.

BOBS

You have probably heard of a bobsled, but do you know what a bob is?

A bob is attached to the back of the sleigh runner, and as long as the sleigh is going forward it just drags. They're useful on a steep hill. If the sleigh starts to slide backwards the bob digs into the snow and stops the sled. Sometimes people used a log or a drag for this purpose.

SLEIGH RUNNER

BOB

GOPHERS

There is nothing you could not do to a prairie dog · · · me and my sister snared them, drowned them, shot them, cut their tails off and sometimes skinned them · · · no one thought anything of it.

GROUND SQUIRRELS

During the depression my grandfather came across a group of men snaring big fat prairie dogs at a colony. They had a few skinned and were roasting them over a fire. He thought they looked awful tempting to tell the truth, but he didn't join them for lunch. While they were talking, he noticed they had snared enough ground squirrels to feed about a hundred men. They were all cleaned and gutted. So they told him a secret. One of them had a job on the railway freighting through to Toronto and Montreal. He would pick up the carcasses and transport them down East where he sold them as a gourmet delicacy; Fresh Ground Squirrel. A butcher down there paid 50 cents apiece so the boys were making more money than they had ever seen before in their lives.

Some months later a Westerner was back East and was invited to share supper fresh from Alberta. He refused to eat prairie dog no matter where it came from. The bottom fell out of the ground squirrel market. People would eat squirrels, but nobody wanted to be caught eating dog meat!

POCKET KNIVES

There's only one kind of jackknife, and that's a German-made item called a Henry Boker. My grandpa, my pa and most of my uncles had one of these knives. The steel in them was soft enough to take an edge quickly and hard enough to keep for a reasonable amount of time and not rust. My grandfather felt that knives with gizzmos were poor substitutes for the tool itself.

SHINGLE ARROWS AND SLINGS

The sling was the important part; we needed an old inner tube, preferably one that wasn't too rotten. We cut off a piece of rubber about 3/4 of an inch wide and maybe a foot and a half long. Today you would probably have to find surgical rubber or hunting elastic. To one end we tied a handle (a piece of broom or willow about 6 inches long) and on the other end we secured a small peg that was a little thicker than a match stick.

To make an arrow from a shingle was easy, you just whittled it out like the pattern and notched the heavy end to accept the small peg on the sling.

This is how it worked: You held the handle in your right hand, elastic up, and you notched the match sized peg into the notch on the shingle arrow. They were not very accurate but we could make 'em fly tremendous distances. Sometimes an uncle took a try and then it seemed that the arrow flew right out of sight, at least a mile!

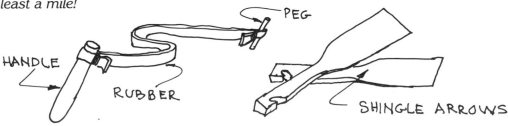

HANDLE   RUBBER   PEG   SHINGLE ARROWS

FIRE CRACKERS

We could buy real fire crackers from the Chinaman's. They came all the way from Hong Kong. You had to ask Woo for them because they weren't sold to kids who were under age.

There were lady fingers, cannon crackers and block busters all wrapped in red crepe. I can still remember him saying to little kids "what you want fire clacker! No way, too young, too young."

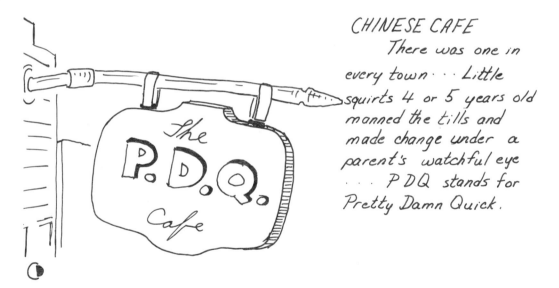

CHINESE CAFE

There was one in every town · · · Little squirts 4 or 5 years old manned the tills and made change under a parent's watchful eye · · · P D Q stands for Pretty Damn Quick.

BLACK POWDER

I used to make black powder with my friend Walter. We always hoped that we would be able to make fire-crackers. We could make it puff or shoot like a rocket but we could never get it to explode with a bang. It is the basis for the powder that was used in long rifles. Here's the formula: three parts sulfur, fifteen parts saltpeter, two parts charcoal, mixed in with a pestle and mortar. We used charcoal briquettes for carbon, the grocer's stock of curing saltpeter, and sulphur picked up along the railway tracks.

THE SWIMMIN' HOLE

We had hundreds along the creek · · · all of them had names · · · the six foot was about three feet deep, the ten foot maybe six. A group of us would walk twenty miles in the sun to swim bare ass in our favorite hole · · ·

NIGGER FISHIN'

We bought small snelled hooks at a penny a piece, number ten thread for line, a willow for a pole. and any bit of wood for a float · · · we sneered at kids who brought store-bought rods · · · they usually never brought them twice.

GOLDEYE

We always felt red-winged grasshoppers were special. We caught and saved them for fishing. First, we took off the outer wings to show the ruby red underwing. Goldeye seemed especially fond of them and we were especially fond of Goldeye. They had much more class than chubs or suckers or carp or jackfish.

If you had a two-pound Goldeye on your line, you knew it. It wasn't that they were really strong fighters. The thing was their bodies were so thin and deep that if they turned cross-ways in the current they were nearly impossible to reel in on a light line. You had to play them carefully. Reel them in when they followed the hook and hold off when they didn't.

CLAMS AND CRAYFISH

I want to say that fresh water clams won't kill you, but they taste as if they might. We kids collected the large ones and chopped, boiled and roasted them. Of course we always claimed to each other and to anyone who would listen that they were delicious.

On the other hand, crayfish really are a treat. When covered with a little salt and butter they taste like fresh lobster. We chased them through the shallows or fished with bits of minnow or liver. There was no need for a hook. Once a crayfish grabs his lunch he doesn't let go and we just pulled them right out of the water.

There isn't much meat on a crayfish. A really big one might have a teaspoon of meat in the tail. Only very young boys and girls have the time to catch enough for a meal.

SINKERS

Most railway bridges have expansion joints in them to prevent spans from bowing in hot weather. The engineers fill these joints with lead. (My pa was the first to show me this wealthy mineral deposit.) If you pry the lead out of the joint with a pocket knife and are able to get a hold of a little copper wire you can go into the sinker business right there under the bridge.

First we would melt the metal in a jam pail pot over a brush fire, then we would poke a stick or a sparrow's egg in the sand to make little weight casting forms. Once the lead was molten we pored it into the sand molds and pushed a copper loop into each one. When they cooled the burrs were bigger than the molds but a pocket knife would trim them off. All the kids in my community did this, so every couple of years the railway engineering department would have to pour us a new supply.

SMOKED FISH

We thought of smoked fish as candy, and liked it more than most sweets. The tougher and stronger it was, the better we liked it. Making it was easy.

You soak the fillets overnight in brine which is a solution of one part salt to one part water. Otherwise just sprinkle salt on the fillets and let them sit. The next day you can smoke them.

SMOKED FISH

Some people have smoke houses. That's fine, but all you really need is a large barrel or tin box. Make a good fire and burn it down to a flameless, smokey glow of coals. Place your fish on sticks or racks in the barrel. The smokey shouldn't have a bottom, only a small vent at the top to let the smoke out. Cover the fire with smoking chips of your choice. (Books written down East say the smoking chips should be hickory or apple. We don't have these on the prairies. You have to use willows which are very strong, or chokecherry twigs which are milder.

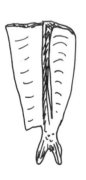

It doesn't take very long, the fish should be removed after an hour or so. Fish prepared like this will last a very long time without spoiling.

People who keep it in the fridge or freeze it don't smoke it as much. They prefer a more subtle smoke flavour. I like it strong and salty and tough.

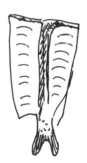

CLAY BAKING

I don't want to make this sound even the least bit complicated. When you're clay baking a fish you don't have to scale it or fillet it. You can clean it if you want to. You simply cover the whole fish in a clay blanket about 1/2" thick, throw it into a fire of just-hot coals, and then cover it. Wait 20 minutes, rake it out and crack the clay off. The clay will take the skin and scales with it. Now you can eat your fish. You can do the same with birds, eggs and small game.

SPORTS DAY

I used to ride my bike to the diamond when it was empty, and visualize the games · · · Everyone practised, and planned and waited for the big tournament · · · this year we'd beat those guys from Crossfield.

HORSE SHOES

You knew you were a man when they let you play · · · women and children were not encouraged. Sunburnt men talked quietly or swore softly, · · · as the heavy shoes soared through the evening air and rang on the steel pegs.

ONE ROOM SCHOOL HOUSE
    You don't know nothin' about the prairie if you
haven't fallen asleep in the cloak room while the fiddle
and piano reeled and folks tromped, danced, ate and
drank, talked and fought till morning.

EGG TOSS

This was my favorite sports-day or picnic competition. Couples faced each other about three feet apart and tossed a raw egg back and forth from one to another. They took a step back from each other after each toss. As the gap widened they had to throw the egg farther and harder. The couple that kept their egg together over the greatest distance won the competition. Everyone else ended up covered with egg yolk or shells. It's surprising how far some folks were able to throw or catch an egg without breaking it.

SPORTS DAY

Foul balls were worth a nickle, so was a hot dog or a slice of watermelon. Orange Crush was a dime and came in a wrinkled brown bottle.

MOUTH MUSIC

A Metis fiddler was a very popular man whether or not he brought a fiddle to the dance. Once he was there he had the responsibility for playing, with or without an instrument. I've seen an old man do a rendition of the Red River Jig by singing de-dil-de de-dil-de de-dil-de sawing an imaginary fiddle and rocking back on an old chair while his feet tapped out a familiar tick-a-tum tick-a-tum tick-a-tum. I've seen Frenchmen, Scots and Irishmen all resort to the same instruments and very effectively too. Who needed a fiddle and a bow? The dancers never even noticed, especially if there were three or four phantom fiddlers playing.

A SIX HOLER

    This hotel is somewhere in the south ··· I can't remember where. We thought it was hilarious ··· and vowed never to use the main floor facilities ···

HOTEL BARS

During the first half of this century many of the hotels were owned and built by the breweries. They had to invest in the establishments in order to get the extra distribution. Most are now owned by small ma and pa proprietors. But in the days when dad was first in the beer parlors you could buy the hotel's own brand of beer and ale.

HALLOWEEN

We did all the usual things, pushed over out-houses, soaped windows, and pushed parked cars into the street. The best trick we pulled was by accident.

The local bicycle cowboys of which I was one discovered a full hay rack behind a farm truck. We unhitched it and hauled it up a hill opposite the hotel. Then we let her go; right into the Ladies and Escorts doorway. Wagon parts and straw exploded at the entrance.

We headed for the hills, the door flew open and half the patrons tumbled out hollering. They made an awful racket, but they only caught a glimpse of us as we high-tailed it out of town.

THE OLDEST (AND POSSIBLY WORST) PRAIRIE JOKE

How do you cook a crane? Well sir, first you fill a kettle with water, throw in a couple of rocks and pluck a good size crane and throw him in too. Then you boil the lot for a couple of days and simmer it for a few more. When the rocks are tender to the fork, you throw away the crane and serve them up with the broth.

Gramp would tell this joke to anyone who cared to listen and to quite a few who didn't. He'd laugh until he'd have to leave the room. For years and years I could not understand this joke.

71

CHURCHES

If there was a hill in town, some one dragged an old granary up there, cut windows in it, put a steeple on it··· and made themselves a church.

THE BUTTE

Once every summer we would visit my uncle's grave and grandma planted bleeding hearts beside it · · · Later, we waited in the car while she stood quietly alone, out in the wind and summer heat.

THE TIPPLE

Every year some one fell down a mine shaft, · · · usually a kid, and usually they died · · · the mines didn't treat the children who played on them any differently than the men who worked them

COAL

    Anywhere there's a river bank on the prairie, there's a coal seam and a mine. They were the perfect place to play··· we stole blasting caps or charges, and looked for old carbide lamps in the refuse··· At night the slack pits burned and glowed in the dark like hills on fire.

THE MINE

Dad started working the mine when he got out of school. By this time it was a dying occupation. He hated it, but it was close to home.

He was assigned a horse, one of those stubborn little Welsh ponies. Its name was Mouse, and he was about as old as the hills dad mined.

Mouse fought daily with dad as they hauled coal through the galleries from the mine face to the tipple. He'd bite and kick him at every opportunity. My dad never dared to drop his guard. If he did Mouse gave him a licking.

One afternoon Mouse wouldn't pull the car into the north gallery. There was really nothing unusual about this. Mouse always refused to go where he was wanted. After trying everything dad gave up, turned him around and took him to the paddock to unharness him. Just then the gallery collapsed. The timber gave and the overburden of clay, rock and water flooded through the mine.

Dad did two things that afternoon. First he went up to the time keeper and drew his pay. Second he let Mouse go. He opened the paddock and chased him out of the pen. The mine manager said "You can't do that!" Dad replied "The hell I can't, I bought the horse!" (He hadn't.)

Dad got another job working for the highways. Mouse died about a week later of old age.

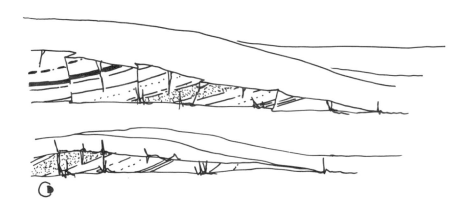

HOO DOOS

We called them bird toilets, ··· because they looked like little earthen outhouses, and because my mother said that's what they called them when she was a kid.

BONE COAL

In a coal seam, petrified wood and sandstone is called bone. A lot of it will make poor quality coal and a banked fire won't last through the night. Once my dad brought home a lump of black bone split in two. It was hollow and all crystallized inside.

ROCKS

Who can break that bottle, bust that telephone insulator or hit that tree? How many times can you skip it on the water, throw it through that hole? If there wasn't something to throw a stone at you just made a pile of them and tried to hit the pile. Kids nowadays with balls and toys of every kind don't realize they're just modern stones.

POLISH POTATOES

Everyone knows that if the stones start coming up once you break land they always will. You can clear them away every year, it doesn't matter. The frost keeps pushing them up and the machinery keeps bringing them to the surface. When a man cultivated in the spring he sometimes thought he was harvesting a crop of stones. Folks in our area called it harvesting the Polish potato crop. Others called them Dutch potatoes, I guess it all depended on on who you were.

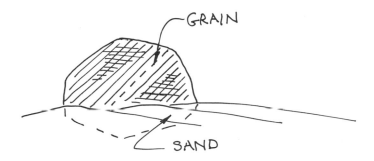

SPLITTING FIELDSTONE

When my Uncle was building his house one of the carpenters he hired was a mason from Saskatchewan. The mason's father's house was completely made from fieldstone granite. One afternoon at coffee-break he showed us how to split the stones. (This is another of those not-talked-about secrets.)

"All granite has a grain" he said, "and that's the only easy place to split it." (You can try to chip it across the grain and sometimes it works, but it's tough going and most of the time the stone just shatters.) So if the stone you've got won't fit when you split it on the grain you'd best get another one.

Now the trick is to find the grain but that's not really hard. Then you take a cold chisel and tap the stone along the grain, all the way around. (It's nice to have a sand pile or a sand table for this because it makes the stone stay in place each time you rotate it.) Keep on tapping the stone and turning it around. Sooner or later it'll split in half along the grain. Usually you don't have to be overly strong or be able to strike the stone with much force. Nearly anyone can do this. There are some people who do it better and that's what makes a craftsman.

TURTLE BACKS

When you see grass growing like this, you
might just as well let it grow · · · it's a solid mass
of vegetation and gumbo · · · it's a good place to
get your horse's leg broke · · ·

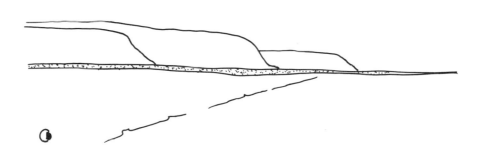

THE HANDHILLS

They always looked like head lands to me · · ·
rising out of the dusty prairie sea. The steppes of
the plains dropping like purple finger tips to the
lower range.

SNAKE HILLS

I know of at least a dozen snake hills. Some spots just attract them. In the Fall they migrate to particular spots by the hundreds. In the Spring they leave again. Some of the unfortunate ones can be seen on the roadways squashed flat, all pointing in the same direction, either all coming or all going.

Once our community had a bad infestation of Fall garter snakes. One of the older boys pulled a prank on one of the old miners. He stripped a willow branch down until nothing but the last two leaves were left on. The old man's privie had no back boards on it at the lower level. When old John went out to use the facilities this kid tickled him with the willow leaf through the hole in the back of the biffy. John took the door right off his little establishment as he lit out of there hollering "SNAKES!!!" with his pants around his knees!

BULL SNAKES

Papa said that bull snakes sometimes ate birds on the prairie. A hungry snake was supposed to be able to lift himself into the air and stay like that, motionless as a dead twig. After a while a little bird might come along and think he was a good place to perch. That's when the snake would strike and have himself a home-delivered meal.

A lot of other folks thought snakes liked to get milk from cows because there would always be a couple of them in the barn. Gramp said that was horse-feathers. I don't know about that, but it's sure they caught a lot of mice in there.

THE DUMP

    My grandfather used his dump as a storehouse. There used to be an old surrey, some grain tanks and heavy wagons parked there, – all of them in good running order. My cousin and I pushed them over the coulee bank · · · I've always regretted doing that.

THE RAINBARREL

  I nearly drowned in ours. · · ·Whats worse is that my grandma always added cow paddies to the water so her peonies would grow better. For awhile after, both the flowers and I grew very well.

THE FORGE

My grandfather had been a smith in his day···
I guess just about every farmer was··· He still
had the forge, but we mostly used acetylene and
the carbon arc.

THE WETSTONE

Gramp kept it in the barn, out of direct sun light. He said the sun would harden it and make it brittle and useless. · · · Whenever he sharpened mower Knives on it, he filled the soup can with water · · · It dripped on the stone as he pumped the foot pedal.

HOW TO MAKE A KNIFE

Almost all our knives were home-made. Old saw blades, spring steel and files could all be made into their own special sort of cutting tool.

I liked to make knives out of old saw blades because they didn't require any special handling. They tended to rust a little, but that was out-weighed by the convenience of not having to treat the slug carefully or temper the final blade.

Prairie homesteaders with little training and less education have been making their own knives for years. The main thing is not to be fooled into thinking that the process is difficult. This is what you do:

1) With a coping saw cut a slug out of a saw blade making it the size and shape you require. (Be careful not to heat the metal up when you cut it.) You can use a dribble of water to keep it cool.

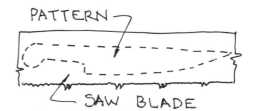

2) Rivet some sort of wooden handle to the blade. Brass rivets are nice to look at but steel or copper ones are probably cheaper and just as good. I like to use an old ash hockey stick for the handle, but most anything will do.

3) Sand down the handle nice and smooth.

4) Put a long taper on the cutting edge of the blade with a file or a grindstone. (Don't let the metal get hot this time either.)

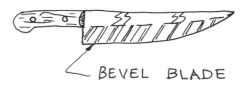

HOW TO MAKE A KNIFE

SLUG   BEVEL   FINISH POINT

5) *Take your pocket stone to it to give it that final sharp edge for cutting.*

Since the saw blade is made out of spring steel it doesn't need any further treatment to make good knife steel. (Just remember, don't over-heat the blade.)

FORGE WELDING

Welding on a forge is a tough job because the blacksmith has to physically pound two hot pieces of metal into one another. Most home smiths knew enough to use borax to make a better job of it. It keeps the air off, making a permanent weld. A charred weld won't hold.

SMITHING

During the 1st World War Grampa went back to fight in the United States Artillery. He was such an excellent blacksmith that he was soon attached to the cavalry remount station.

Forty years later he was still making tools and shoeing horses for neighbours.

Once he made a ring from a horse shoe nail for my sister but he wouldn't make one for me.

WOOD STAIN

Some of the best prairie secrets are so simple and effective that the problem is believing something so uncomplicated could possibly work. Here is an old recipe for wood stain and finish that a friend passed on to me. I've used it many times. On pine wood it's the nicest finish I've ever seen. Just scrape some rust off an old implement into two parts boiled linseed oil and one part of methylhydrate (wood alcohol or gas line anti-freeze will do).

SHELLAC

Once gramps took me down to the Sunset store and we bought some real shellac. This stuff was hard little powdery amber balls; gramps said it came from a kind of bug that lived on the trees in India. He mixed this with wood spirits to make shellac and had a lot of different ways of putting it on things.

One time we also got a can of water stain. It's for staining wood, not coloring water, as I first thought. It was called water stain because you mixed it with water to use it. This really worked on unsized wood. Sometimes the wood absorbed the dye up to an eighth of an inch!

LEATHER HINGES

Not everyone could afford to buy fancy metal hinges from the hardware. It wasn't unusual to see coal bins, wood-sheds and even houses with homemade leather hinges. I remember some folks tooled theirs so they looked quite attractive. But they were practical too. You could bet a leather hinge that ran the height of the door wasn't about to let any draft in!

LONG HORNS

I had to do this, cliché or not · · · I've never seen a longhorn in my life. We always had white faced or red polled herefords · · ·

WINDMILL

    My grandad and uncles used to hunt the old cattle leases east of Drumheller · · · There was nothing but prairie for miles and miles · · · Windmills and stock tanks were about the only signs of human existence; - that and the fences strung forever into the distance.

THE WELL PUMP

Mostly I remember hauling water from a good
well in town · · · a nickel a five gallon bucket · · ·
in the winter the cold frosty pails steamed in the
night air · · ·

DIVINING

The only thing more important than soil and sun, out on the prairie, is water. Some men became famous for their ability to find it.

When you're living on land without trees a clump of willow means water is not far below, but a poplar bluff doesn't mean a thing. If wild poplars are growing there you don't need to dig for water, you should be able to see it. The problem is that farmers and cattlemen have planted poplars in lots of places where they don't normally grow. Although a single tree won't survive, a break of poplars will trap and hold water enough to keep them nice and healthy. But there isn't any water beneath them.

Another sign of water is a line of sage-brush that stands out from the hill. It can look a little like it's flowing itself. There might be water in that line down about 25 or 35 feet which is how far down a sage root can go. Farmers resort to all sorts of gadgets for divining a well: horse hair and a button, willow wands, special hats and shoes; all kinds of things.

Here is one anyone can do, though some folks are luckier than others. Take two clothes hangers and straighten them out, then bend down one end of each to make a sort of handle about one foot long. Now you are ready to witch a well.

DIVINING

Hold each wand loosely in one hand and pointing in front of you. Now start walking. (I've seen people take their shoes off for this, but you don't have to.) When you get close to a running underground stream the wands will cross themselves. If you back-up they will uncross and if you walk further they will try to swing through your body. Pound a peg where the wands cross.

Take the wands and walk slowly toward the spot again, this time from a new direction. Sooner or later the wires will cross again. Pound a peg here too. (The distance between these two spots may prove to be the width of the underground stream.) Now move to the right or left of these sightings and do the whole thing over. Eventually you will be able to peg out the stream of water that's under the ground. Where the stream is widest and the reaction strongest is the place to drill the well. If you're curious about which direction the water flows, walk toward the stream with a single wand. It will swing the same way as the water runs. One problem with this method is that it will locate gas lines and water lines, as well as old car bodies and iron ore deposits. So if you find your stream is about one inch thick or ten feet square, better try again.

ARTESIAN WELLS

A spring that flows unasked out of the ground has a special magic in a country where water is so hard to come by. We didn't have one; gramp's well was over 200 feet deep. Before it was drilled they relied on the slough.

FARMHOUSES

    The one closest to the road is always the son's, and dad and grandpa built the two storey. The chicken coop was probably gramp's first frame house, and somewhere in the back is an old over grown hole or dirt pile · · · the first sod shack.

THE ICEHOUSE

There was still an icehouse on the farm · · ·
it was extremely old and rotten. Wet coal slack
covered the floor · · · it had been used to insulate
the ice · · · On the bald headed prairie, coal slack
was cheaper than sawdust.

CUTTING ICE FROM THE RIVER

If you want ice in the summer you've got to get it in the winter.

When I was young there were no lakes close by so we always cut ice from the river. This was dangerous because the water was moving. If you fell in the current just naturally pulled you under the ice. Without quick help they never found you again. In some places the ice froze nearly to the bottom of the river. Then if you fell in and stood up you might only be wet to the waist. But there was no way to tell this beforehand.

The ferry man was the ice expert in our area. He usually did the cutting. He and his son worked the river together, using a minimum of tools because everything got wet and froze.

They liked to find a spot where the current wasn't too fast, and they looked for ice 18 to 24 inches thick. If it was any thicker the blocks would be too heavy to handle.

He would start by chipping a ramp from the surface down to the floor of the ice cap. Then they cut blocks into rectangles about three feet by four feet. The blocks were then manoeuvered to the ramp and flipped on their sides with pike poles. Then one of them would bob the block by pushing down hard on the block and then letting up quickly. This made the ice sort of pop up or bob out of the water. When it was high enough to clear the bottom of the ramp the son bulled it up the slope with a pair of ice tongs.

They had a ramp built up to the height of the sleigh bed and just pushed the block right in.

It was hard to appreciate the coldness of the work when everyone was soaked and frozen, but in the summertime, the ice was a big treat.

CUTTING ICE

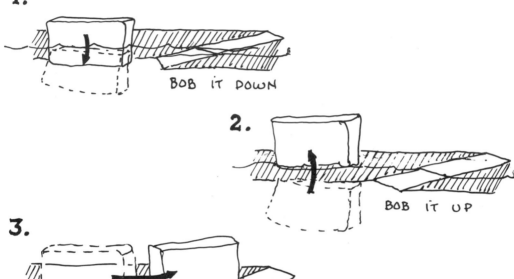

1.

BOB IT DOWN

2.

BOB IT UP

3.

PULL IT OUT

ICE PITS

People who were too poor to build ice houses or didn't live near a river or a slough made a supply of summer ice in an ice pit. They dug pits into the ground anywhere from 10 to 15 feet deep. After the ground was frozen they would haul water into it. They only filled a little at a time (no more than six to eight inches) so each successive layer froze until the whole pit would be frozen solid with ice. If they had filled it full of water from the first only the top few feet would ever have frozen. The really great thing about the pit was that the ice thawed away from the sides in the summer and a deep column of ice was left standing in water. The best pits were lined with gunny sacks or canvas and topped over with a wooden roof and hay bales or straw. This made the water cleaner and it lasted well through the summer.

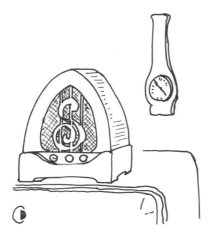

THE RADIO

    The radio sat on the ice box · · · gramps would let it be turned on for three things ; the grain and stock market reports, the weather, and the Amos and Andy Show · · ·

THE PARTYLINE

Sometimes there was as many as 18 families on a line. Anytime anyone got a call, everyone else knew it cause it rang in all 18 houses. Each ring was a code · · · Grandma's was "two shorts and a long."